Saints and Lodgers

W.H. Davies (1871-1940) was born in Newport. In his twenties, he spent several years moving around America as a beggar, leaping on and off moving trains to get around, ultimately leading to the loss of his right leg in a train accident. *The Autobiography of a Super-tramp*, which chronicles these experiences, was published in 1908. *The Soul's Destroyer and Other Poems*, his first collection of verse, drawing on his experiences of a down-and-out existence in London lodging houses, was published in 1905. Supported and celebrated by literary figures such as Edward Thomas and George Bernard Shaw, as well as the *Georgian Poetry* anthology series, Davies published more than twenty volumes of poetry, as well as works of fiction and non-fiction. *Young Emma*, an account of his courtship of his wife Helen Payne, was published posthumously in 1980. Though he is most famous as a poet for his much-anthologised 'Leisure,' which celebrates an ideal of rural life, *Saints and Lodgers* gives us the wider range of Davies's poetic concerns, focusing in particular on the gritty social realism of the poems drawn from his experiences of poverty.

Jonathan Edwards is from Crosskeys, near Newport. His first collection of poems, *My Family and Other Superheroes*, received the Costa Po-etry Award and the Wales Book of the Year People's Choice Award. It was short-listed for the Fenton Aldeburgh First Collection Prize. His second collection, *Gen*, also received the Wales Book of the Year People's Choice Award, and in 2019 his poem about Newport Bridge was shortlisted for the Forward Prize for Best Single Poem.

Saints and Lodgers

Poems of W. H. Davies

Selected with an introduction by
Jonathan Edwards

PARTHIAN

On receiving an unsolicited copy of 'The Soul's Destroyer', W.H Davies's first collection, by George Bernard Shaw

"There were no author's compliments, no publisher's compliments, indeed no publisher in the ordinary channel of the trade in minor poetry. The author, as far as I could guess, had walked into a printer's or stationer's shop; handed in his manuscript; and ordered his book as he might have ordered a pair of boots. It was marked "price half a crown." An accompanying letter asked me very civilly if I required a half-crown book of verses; and if so, would I please send the author the half-crown; if not, would I return the book. This was attractively simple and sensible."

Cover Artist of Pigeon Loft and Mine
George Little was born in the east end of Swansea in 1927 he grew up next to the abandoned copperworks, slag heaps and still-busy docks of Dylan Thomas's 'ugly, lovely town'. As a teenager the destruction of the Swansea Blitz was seared into his imagination. He trained at Swansea College of Art and the Ruskin School of Drawing in Oxford and lectured in art history at Swansea University. George Little brought a deep visual knowledge to a life's work exploring the dramatic forms and startling colours of industrial and urban decay in photographs, drawings and paintings. He continued working until his death in 2019. 'George Little: The Ugly Lovely Landscape' by Peter Wakelin was published in 2023.

Parthian, Cardigan SA43 1ED
First published in 2020 Reprinted 2024
The copyright of the introduction and the selection remains with Jonathan Edwards
ISBN 978-1-914595-68-4 Typeset by Elaine Sharples
Printed and bound by 4edge Limited, UK
Cover image: Pigeon Loft and Mine by George Little
Cover design: Marc Jennings
Published with the financial support of the Welsh Books Council
British Library Cataloguing in Publication Data
A cataloguing record for this book is available from the British Library

CONTENTS

Introduction

There's something very odd in Newport. Lots of people would say, of course, that there are lots of very odd things in Newport, but I'm referring here to one thing in particular. There, at the bottom of the main street, surrounded by shoppers flouncing home from Next and Poundland, and other folk falling out of the nearby Wetherspoons, a dark figure stands. Half man, half tree, its face covered with a sculpted handkerchief, a necessary plaque tells you what it is: a statue in memory of W. H. Davies.

It was years, though, before I knew that. I walk past that statue most writing days, on my way from one Newport café to another, muttering under my breath a stanza or line from the latest draft of a poem. But it was only after years of doing this that someone pointed out to me what that statue was. No one would figure this surrealist thing, which must have been conceived on a day when the artist was either especially inspired or – fittingly, given Davies's interests – especially drunk, as a statue of the poet, who is, above all, a writer of the real rather than the imagined. Once I did know it, I began occasionally saluting the statue on my way past, and it even made its way into a few poems. Sometimes I even felt that it was waving back or tipping me the wink, that Davies knew what I was up to or was cheering me on. When poets from India visited and I treated them to the Literary Highlights of Gwent tour (a short tour, it must be said), the first step was to read some of Davies's poems in front of that statue.

So who was Davies and what was *he* up to? Born in Newport in 1871, he travelled around America and Canada as a hobo, jumping on and off moving trains as a way of getting round the country, a means of transport which had the advantage of cheapness and the disadvantage of being bloody dangerous. He eventually lost a leg in the process – these extraordinary experiences are documented in his famous prose work, *The Autobiography of a Super-tramp*. He lived a pauper's existence in lodging houses in London, and was so desperate to become a writer that at one point he hawked his printed poems from door to door. Incredibly – and for those wanting evidence of the miraculous, here you might find it – his commitment paid off, his writing was discovered and brought him great fame, with press photographers turning up to the lodging house – one might imagine the modern equivalent, of a bloke living on the streets of London becoming a literary star overnight, and being hounded by the paparazzi. From there on, he was a prolific writer in poetry and prose, managing the further miracle of supporting himself by writing. In his fifties, he married Helen Payne, almost thirty years his junior, who he had met while out on one of his not infrequent searches for prostitutes – experiences documented in the posthumously published *Young Emma*. They lived in rural contentment for the last twenty years of Davies's life, as he continued to write and publish in volume.

So far, so Hollywood-friendly. There are grounds for arguing that every writer should live such an exciting life, particularly in this era of the writer-as-creative-writing-academic. But what about the poems such a life produced? Beyond 'Leisure,' which anthologies, teachers and – God help us – adverts have kept in people's minds, how many of us know much about Davies's verse? When I was approached to edit a selection of his poems, it was, to my shame, an opportunity to acquaint myself with the work of a writer from just down the road.

The poems I've selected from Davies's work might in some ways seem like an eccentric choice, though in fairness, to work on the poems of someone like Davies, eccentricity might seem like a good qualification. I'm no Davies scholar and my interest here hasn't been to compile a volume for scholars or which is necessarily representative of the enormous body of Davies's published poems. The place to go for that is Jonathan Barker's *Selected Poems*, and I would also recommend the 1963 Cape edition of *The Complete Poems*. What I've been after is a readerly edition. I wanted to put before the reader the poems I've found most affecting and important, and to sequence them in a way that showed them to their best advantage. Given my interests, it is inevitable that the Davies presented here will be skewed slightly. Of course, the poems about Wales are here. Where Davies praises Twmbarlwm, Allt-yr-yn and Malpas Brook, he's writing poems that I want to survive, about places I've climbed or sighed or lurked in. As a former teacher, one of the reasons for my interest in Davies is that many people will be growing up now in those places not knowing that they have been written about in that way, or that they *can* be written about.

For me, one of the most exciting things about Davies which emerged in this reading is his social realism, his commitment to writing about a turn-of-the-twentieth-century, down-and-out existence, portraying tramps and prostitutes – the lodging house folk he lived amongst. Faced with these poems, a case can be made for Davies's work as important and ahead of its time. His desire to write sympathetically and unsentimentally about these lives, in accessible and simple poems, means that it is possible to draw an admittedly very wobbly (and probably, in Davies's case, beer-fuelled) line to his work from aspects of Blake's, and from his work to the poems of writers like Charles Bukowski and Simon Armitage. Davies loved his garden, and he loved nature, and there are many pages of his *Complete Poems* where you will find Another Bloody Poem About Birds. But for me, where it's been possible to drop such poems in favour of his writing about people, I've done that.

One question I've been thinking about as I've been doing this work has been whether it's been worth doing. A selected Davies hasn't appeared since 1985, *The Complete Poems* is out of print, and recent anthologies of the prose and poetry – Rory Waterman's *The True Traveller* is an exemplary introduction to the range of the prose – tend to go light on the verse. One edition of his collected poems is published by an imprint called Forgotten Books. There's an argument of course that says that if poems don't survive it's because they don't deserve to, though it doesn't take much exposure to the vagaries and complexities of the publishing industry to know that this is, roughly, horse's codswallop. One issue is that Davies is not a poet of formal range, and the forms he frequently employed – *tuh boom tuh boom tuh boom RHYME!* – have dated. His poems are sometimes short and simply don't go very far. A commercially successful poet, he bashed out book after book, and there is a feeling in his writing that he's publishing absolutely everything he has to hand – something which would destroy any poet. Yet Edward Thomas championed his writing and helped him financially, and Dylan Thomas included poems by him when giving readings. Anything that's good enough for those writers will do for me.

Whatever questions I have are ultimately resolved by the care for people in the best of these poems, the tender recording of lives and experiences poetry often turns from, which renders the poems important. So much of why I write my own poems is tied up with that. And more than that, there's how I feel every time I pass that statue in Newport, like it knows what I'm struggling for, like it's laughing its arse off in affection or mick-take. So here's a book for W. H. Davies, for new readers to perform from while standing in front of his statue, or to shout from, above the noise of a jukebox in a Newport pub, or the sound of traffic rushing past a shop doorway at night. Or, indeed, to carry in your pocket as you walk past that statue, the people of Newport bustling around you and, if you must, one bird circling above. To carry in your breast pocket, say, near your heart, as you offer that statue a salute, and a line of your latest poem suddenly shouts in your ear, or buzzes like something, there on your lips.

Jonathan Edwards

I am the Poet Davies, William

I am the Poet Davies, William,
    I sin without a blush or blink:
I am a man that lives to eat;
    I am a man that lives to drink.

My face is large, my lips are thick,
    My skin is coarse and black almost;
But the ugliest feature is my verse,
    Which proves my soul is black and lost.

Thank heaven thou didst not marry me,
    A poet full of blackest evil;
For how to manage my damned soul
    Will puzzle many a flaming devil.

The East in Gold

Somehow this world is wonderful at times,
    As it has been from early morn in May;
Since first I heard the cock-a-doodle-do—
    Timekeeper on green farms – at break of day.

Soon after that I heard ten thousand birds,
    Which made me think an angel brought a bin
Of golden grain, and none was scattered yet—
    To rouse those birds that make that merry din.

I could not sleep again, for such wild cries,
    And went out early into their green world;
And then I saw what set their little tongues
    To scream for joy – they saw the East in gold.

Songs of Joy

Sing out, my Soul, thy songs of joy;
    Such as a happy bird will sing
Beneath a Rainbow's lovely arch
    In early spring.

Think not of Death in thy young days;
    Why shouldst thou that grim tyrant fear,
And fear him not when thou art old,
    And he is near.

Strive not for gold, for greedy fools
    Measure themselves by poor men never;
Their standard still being richer men,
    Makes them poor ever.

Train up thy mind to feel content,
    What matters then how low thy store;
What we enjoy, and not possess,
    Makes rich or poor.

Filled with sweet thought, then happy I
    Take not my state from others' eyes;
What's in my mind – not on my flesh
    Or theirs – I prize.

Sing, happy Soul, thy songs of joy;
    Such as a Brook sings in the wood,
That all night has been strengthened by
    Heaven's purer flood.

A Beggar's Life

When farmers sweat and toil at ploughs,
   Their wives give me cool milk and sweet;
When merchants in their office brood,
   Their ladies give me cakes to eat,
And hot tea for my happy blood;
    This is a jolly life indeed,
    To do no work and get my need.

I have no child for future thought,
   I feed no belly but my own,
And I can sleep when toilers fail;
   Content, though sober, sleeps on stone,
But Care can't sleep with down and ale;
    This is a happy life indeed,
    To do no work and get my need.

I trouble not for pauper's grave,
   There is no feeling after death;
The king will be as deaf to praise
   As I to blame – when this world saith
A word of us in after days;
    It is a jolly life indeed,
    To do no work and get my need.

Leisure

What is this life if, full of care,
We have no time to stand and stare.

No time to stand beneath the boughs
And stare as long as sheep or cows.

No time to see, when woods we pass,
Where squirrels hide their nuts in grass.

No time to see, in broad daylight,
Streams full of stars, like skies at night.

No time to turn at Beauty's glance,
And watch her feet, how they can dance.

No time to wait till her mouth can
Enrich that smile her eyes began.

A poor life this if, full of care,
We have no time to stand and stare.

Love Absent

Where wert thou, love, when from Twm Barlum turned
   The moon's face full the way of Alteryn,
And from his wood's dark cage the nightingale
   Drave out clear notes across the open sheen?

I stood alone to see the ripples run
   From light to shade, and shade to light, in play;
Like fearsome children stealing guilty moves
   When Age is dozing – when thou wert away.

The banks of Alteryn are no less sweet,
   Nor Malpas Brook more chary of his flowers,
And I unchanged as they; but thou, dear love,
   Allowest Time to part us with his hours.

Days that have Been

Can I forget the sweet days that have been,
　　When poetry first began to warm my blood;
When from the hills of Gwent I saw the earth
　　Burned into two by Severn's silver flood:

When I would go alone at night to see
　　The moonlight, like a big white butterfly,
Dreaming on that old castle near Caerleon,
　　While at its side the Usk went softly by:

When I would stare at lovely clouds in Heaven,
　　Or watch them when reported by deep streams;
When feeling pressed like thunder, but would not
　　Break into that grand music of my dreams?

Can I forget the sweet days that have been,
　　The villages so green I have been in;
Llantarnam, Magor, Malpas, and Llanwern,
　　Liswery, old Caerleon, and Alteryn?

Can I forget the banks of Malpas Brook,
　　Or Ebbw's voice in such a wild delight,
As on he dashed with pebbles in his throat,
　　Gurgling towards the sea with all his might?

Ah, when I see a leafy village now,
　　I sigh and ask it for Llantarnam's green;
I ask each river where is Ebbw's voice—
　　In memory of the sweet days that have been.

The River Severn

This is the morning bright and clear,
    To stand on top of Christchurch Hill;
We'll see the Severn, looking down,
    In all his silver beauty, Love—
Where he lies basking in the sun.

My lovely Severn shines as bright
    As any moon on trucks of coal,
Or sun above our greenest meadow;
    Till I again defy the world
To search his face and find a shadow.

The Mind's Liberty

The mind, with its own eyes and ears,
    May for these others have no care;
No matter where this body is,
    The mind is free to go elsewhere.
My mind can be a sailor, when
    This body's still confined to land;
And turn these mortals into trees,
    That walk in Fleet Street or the Strand.

So, when I'm passing Charing Cross,
    Where porters work both night and day,
I ofttimes hear sweet Malpas Brook,
    That flows thrice fifty miles away.
And when I'm passing near St Paul's,
    I see, beyond the dome and crowd,
Twm Barlum, that green pap in Gwent,
    With its dark nipple in a cloud.

Old Acquaintance

Thy water, Alteryn,
Shines brighter through my tears,
With childhood in my mind:
So will it shine when age
Has made me almost blind.

How canst thou look so young
On my fast changing flesh
And brooding cares that kill—
Oh, you sweet witch as fresh
And fair as childhood – still?

The Villain

While joy gave clouds the light of stars,
    That beamed where'er they looked;
And calves and lambs had tottering knees,
    Excited, while they sucked;
While every bird enjoyed his song,
Without one thought of harm or wrong—
I turned my head and saw the wind,
    Not far from where I stood,
Dragging the corn by her golden hair,
    Into a dark and lonely wood.

The Dragonfly

Now, when my roses are half buds, half flowers,
    And loveliest, the king of flies has come—
It was a fleeting visit, all too brief;
    In three short minutes he had seen them all,
And rested, too, upon an apple leaf.

There, his round shoulders humped with emeralds,
    A gorgeous opal crown set on his head,
And all those shining honours to his breast—
    'My garden is a lovely place,' thought I,
'But is it worthy of so fine a guest?'

He rested there, upon that apple leaf—
    'See, see,' I cried amazed, 'his opal crown,
And all those emeralds clustered round his head!'
    'His breast, my dear, how lovely was his breast'—
The voice of my Beloved quickly said.

'See, see his gorgeous crown, that shines
    With all those jewels bulging round its rim'—
I cried aloud at night, in broken rest.
    Back came the answer quickly, in my dream—
'His breast, my dear, how lovely was his breast!'

The Kingfisher

It was the Rainbow gave thee birth,
   And left thee all her lovely hues;
And, as her mother's name was Tears,
   So runs it in thy blood to choose
For haunts the lonely pools, and keep
In company with trees that weep.

Go you and, with such glorious hues,
   Live with proud Peacocks in green parks;
On lawns as smooth as shining glass,
   Let every feather show its marks;
Get thee on boughs and clap thy wings
Before the windows of proud kings.

Nay, lovely Bird, thou art not vain;
   Thou hast no proud, ambitious mind;
I also love a quiet place
   That's green, away from all mankind;
A lonely pool, and let a tree
Sigh with her bosom over me.

Robin Redbreast

Robin on a leafless bough,
   Lord in Heaven, how he sings!
Now cold Winter's cruel Wind
   Makes playmates of poor, dead things.

How he sings for joy this morn!
   How his breast doth pant and glow!
Look you how he stands and sings,
   Half-way up his legs in snow!

If these crumbs of bread were pearls,
   And I had no bread at home,
He should have them for that song;
   Pretty Robin Redbreast, Come.

The Hawk

Thou dost not fly, thou art not perched,
   The air is all around:
What is it that can keep thee set,
   From falling to the ground?
The concentration of thy mind
   Supports thee in the air;
As thou dost watch the small young birds,
   With such a deadly care.

My mind has such a hawk as thou,
   It is an evil mood;
It comes when there's no cause for grief,
   And on my joys doth brood.
Then do I see my life in parts;
   The earth receives my bones,
The common air absorbs my mind—
   It knows not flowers from stones.

Sweet Stay-at-Home

Sweet Stay-at-Home, sweet Well-content,
Thou knowest of no strange continent:
Thou hast not felt thy bosom keep
A gentle motion with the deep;
Thou hast not sailed in Indian seas,
Where scent comes forth in every breeze.
Thou hast not seen the rich grape grow
For miles, as far as eyes can go;
Thou hast not seen a summer's night
When maids could sew by a worm's light;
Nor the North Sea in spring send out
Bright hues that like birds flit about
In solid cages of white ice—
Sweet Stay-at-Home, sweet Love-one-place.
Thou hast not seen black fingers pick
White cotton when the bloom is thick,
Nor heard black throats in harmony;
Nor hast thou sat on stones that lie
Flat on the earth, that once did rise
To hide proud kings from common eyes;
Thou hast not seen plains full of bloom
Where green things had such little room
They pleased the eye like fairer flowers—
Sweet Stay-at-Home, all these long hours.
Sweet Well-content, sweet Love-one-place,
Sweet, simple maid, bless thy dear face;
For thou hast made more homely stuff
Nurture thy gentle self enough;
I love thee for a heart that's kind—
Not for the knowledge in thy mind.

The Bed-sitting-room

Must I live here, with Scripture on my walls,
Death-cards with rocks and anchors; on my shelf
Plain men and women with plain histories
A proud landlady knows, and no one else?
Let me have pictures of a richer kind:
Scenes in low taverns, with their beggar rogues
Singing and drinking ale; who buy more joy
With a few pence than others can with pounds.
Show gipsies on wild commons, camped at fires
Close to their caravans; where they cook flesh
They have not bought, and plants not sold to them.
Show me the picture of a drinking monk
With his round belly like a mare in foal,
Belted, to keep his guts from falling out
When he laughs hearty; or a maid's bare back,
Who teases me with a bewitching smile
Thrown over her white shoulder. Let me see
The picture of a sleeping damosel,
Who has a stream of shining hair to fill
Up that deep channel banked by her white breasts.
Has Beauty never smiled from off these walls,
Has Genius never entered in a book?
Nay, Madam, keep your room; for in my box
I have a lovely picture of young Eve,
Before she knew what sewing was. Alas!
If I hung on your wall her naked form,
Among your graves and crosses, Scripture texts,
Your death-cards with their anchors and their rocks—
What then? I think this life a joyful thing,
And, like a bird that sees a sleeping cat,
I leave with haste your death-preparing room.

The Start

When dogs play in the sun outdoors,
   And cats chase sunbeams on the mat;
When merry maidens laugh for joy,
   And young men cock their ears at that;
And babes can see in panes of glass
A better light than firegrate has;

When to my teeth ale is not cold,
   And sweeter than hot toast is bread;
When I, no longer charmed by books,
   Seek human faces in their stead;
And every stranger that I meet
Will seem a friend whom I must greet;

When I no sooner up at morn,
   Must like a turkey bolt my food,
To tramp the white green-bordered roads,
   And hear birds sing in many a wood:
When such a time of year has come,
The whole wide world can be my home.

Come, let us Find

Come, let us find a cottage, love,
　　That's green for half a mile around;
To laugh at every grumbling bee,
　　Whose sweetest blossom's not yet found.
Where many a bird shall sing for you,
　　And in our garden build its nest:
They'll sing for you as though their eggs
　　Were lying in your breast,
　　　　　My love—
　　Were lying warm in your soft breast.

'Tis strange how men find time to hate,
　　When life is all too short for love;
But we, away from our own kind,
　　A different life can live and prove.
And early on a summer's morn,
　　As I go walking out with you,
We'll help the sun with our warm breath
　　To clear away the dew,
　　　　　My love,
　　To clear away the morning dew.

The Lodging House Fire

My birthday – yesterday,
Its hours were twenty-four;
Four hours I lived lukewarm,
And killed a score.

Eight bells and then I woke,
Came to our fire below,
Then sat four hours and watched
Its sullen glow.

Then out four hours I walked,
The lukewarm four I live,
And felt no other joy
Than air can give.

My mind durst know no thought,
It knew my life too well:
'Twas hell before, behind,
And round me hell.

Back to that fire again,
Ten hours I watch it now,
And take to bed dim eyes
And fever's brow.

Ten hours I give to sleep,
More than my need, I know;
But I escape my mind
And that fire's glow.

For listen: it is death
To watch that fire's glow;
For, as it burns more red
Men paler grow.

O better in foul room
That's warm, make life away,
Than homeless out of doors,
Cold night and day.

Pile on the coke, make fire,
Rouse its death-dealing glow;
Men are borne dead away
Ere they can know.

I lie; I cannot watch
Its glare from hour to hour;
It makes one sleep, to wake
Out of my power.

I close my eyes and swear
It shall not wield its power;
No use, I wake to find
A murdered hour

Lying between us there!
That fire drowsed me deep,
And I wrought murder's deed—
Did it in sleep.

I count us, thirty men,
Huddled from Winter's blow,
Helpless to move away
From that fire's glow.

So goes my life each day—
Its hours are twenty-four—
Four hours I live lukewarm,
And kill a score.

No man lives life so wise
But unto Time he throws
Morsels to hunger for
At his life's close.

Were all such morsels heaped—
Time greedily devours,
When man sits still – he'd mourn
So few wise hours.

But all my day is waste,
I live a lukewarm four
And make a red coke fire
Poison the score.

Saints and Lodgers

Ye saints, that sing in rooms above,
Do ye want souls to consecrate?
Here's 'Boosy' Bob, 'Pease Pudding' Joe,
And 'Fishy Fat,' of Billingsgate.

Such language only they can speak,
It juggles heaven and hell together;
One threatens, with a fearful oath,
To slit a nose like a pig's trotter.

Here's sporting Fred, swears he is robbed,
And out of fifteen shillings done
By his own pal, who would not lend
Sixpence to back a horse that won.

Here's Davie, he's so used to drink,
When sober he is most bemuddled;
He steers his craft with better skill,
And grows quite sly when he is fuddled.

Here's 'Brummy' Tom, a little man,
Who proudly throws his weight in drink;
He knows men think him poor when sober,
And then, ashamed, to bed doth slink.

The 'Masher' who, by his kind deeds,
The friendship of our house hath lost;
He lent out cash that's not repaid—
They hate him worst who owe him most.

Here's 'Irish' Tim, outspoken wretch,
Insult him, he is thy staunch friend;
But say 'Good morning,' civil like,
He'll damn thee then to thy life's end.

What use are friends if not to bear
Our venom and malicious spleen!
Which, on our life! we dare not give
To foes who'll question what we mean.

Come down, ye saints, to old 'Barge' Bill,
And make his wicked heart to quake,
His stomach nothing can upset,
He boils his tea an hour to make.

Ye saints above, come to these sinners:
To 'Sunny' James, and 'Skilly' Bob,
'The Major,' 'Dodger,' 'Tinker' George,
And 'Deafy,' he's the lodgers' snob.

Here's 'Yank,' we call 'All Legs and Wings,'
He's so erratic in his motion;
And poor wee 'Punch,' a sickly man—
He's worse when he hath ta'en his lotion.

'Haymaker' George, a pig for pickles,
And 'Brass' for old clay pipes swops new;
Here's 'Balmy' Joe, he's cursed clean,
Sweeps beetles in one's mutton stew.

'Australian' Bill, ta'en sick away,
Came home to find his wife hath slid
To other arms; he's done with Liz,
But in his heart he wants the kid.

Here's Jack, so mean he begs from beggars,
Who make scant living door to door;
Here's 'Slim,' a quiet man awake,
Whose sleep's a twenty-horse-power snore.

Here's 'Sailor,' pacing to and fro,
Twice on his four hours' watch to see;
Ten paces forward, ten go aft—
A silent man and mystery.

'The Watchman' takes twelve naps a day
And at each wake his mouth is foul;
When he shall wake from his last sleep
He'll have good cause to curse his soul.

Here's gentle Will, who knows most things,
Throws light on Egypt and the Nile—
And many more to consecrate,
If, Christian folk, ye think worth while.

Toy-sellers, fish-men, paper-men,
A few work barges, few are cadgers;
Some make up flowers from wire and wool,
Some pensions take – such are our lodgers.

Australian Bill

Australian Bill is dying fast,
    For he's a drunken fool:
He either sits in an alehouse,
    Or stands outside a school.

He left this house of ours at seven,
    And he was drunk by nine;
And when I passed him near a school
    He nods his head to mine.

When Bill took to the hospital,
    Sick, money he had none—
He came forth well, but lo! his home,
    His wife and child had gone.

'I'll watch a strange school every day,
    Until the child I see;
For Liz will send the child to school—
    No doubt of that,' says he.

And 'Balmy' Tom is near as bad,
    A-drinking ale till blind:
No absent child grieves he, but there's
    A dead love on his mind.

But Bill, poor Bill, is dying fast,
    For he's the greater fool;
He either sits in an alehouse
    Or stands outside a school.

The Blind Boxer

He goes with basket and slow feet,
To sell his nuts from street to street;
The very terror of his kind,
Till blackened eyes had made him blind.
For this is Boxer Bob, the man
That had hard muscles, harder than
A schoolboy's bones; who held his ground
When six tall bullies sparred around.
Small children now, that have no grace,
Can steal his nuts before his face;
And, when he threatens with his hands,
Mock him two feet from where he stands;
Mock him who could, some years ago
Have leapt five feet to strike a blow.
Poor Bobby, I remember when
Thou wert a god to drunken men;
But now they push thee off, or crack
Thy nuts and give no money back.
They swear they'll strike thee in the face,
Dost thou not hurry from that place;
Such are the men that once would pay
To keep thee drunk from day to day.
With all thy strength and cunning skill,
Thy courage, lasting breath, and will,
Thou'rt helpless now; a little ball,
No bigger than a cherry small,
Has now refused to guide and lead
Twelve stone of strong, hard flesh that need
But that ball's light to make thee leap
And strike these cowards down like sheep.
Poor, helpless Bobby, blind: I see
Thy working face and pity thee.

The Heap of Rags

One night when I went down
Thames' side, in London Town,
A heap of rags saw I,
And sat me down close by.
That thing could shout and bawl,
But showed no face at all;
When any steamer passed
And blew a loud shrill blast,
That heap of rags would sit
And make a sound like it;
When struck the clock's deep bell,
It made those peals as well.
When winds did moan around,
It mocked them with that sound;
When all was quiet, it
Fell into a strange fit;
Would sigh, and moan, and roar,
It laughed, and blessed, and swore.
Yet that poor thing, I know,
Had neither friend nor foe;
Its blessing or its curse
Made no one better or worse.
I left it in that place—
The thing that showed no face.
Was it a man that had
Suffered till he went mad?
So many showers and not
One rainbow in the lot;
Too many bitter fears
To make a pearl from tears.

The Sleepers

As I walked down the waterside
   This silent morning, wet and dark;
Before the cocks in farmyards crowed,
   Before the dogs began to bark;
Before the hour of five was struck
By old Westminster's mighty clock:

As I walked down the waterside
   This morning, in the cold damp air,
I saw a hundred women and men
   Huddled in rags and sleeping there:
These people have no work, thought I,
And long before their time they die.

That moment, on the waterside,
   A lighted car came at a bound;
I looked inside, and saw a score
   Of pale and weary men that frowned;
Each man sat in a huddled heap,
Carried to work while fast asleep.

Ten cars rushed down the waterside,
   Like lighted coffins in the dark;
With twenty dead men in each car,
   That must be brought alive by work:
These people work too hard, thought I,
And long before their time they die.

Saturday Night in the Slums

Why do I stare at faces, why,
  Nor watch the happy children more?
Since Age has now a blackened eye,
  And that grey hair is stained with gore.

For an old woman passed, and she
  Would hide her face when I did stare,
But when she turns that face from me,
  There's clotted blood in her grey hair.

Aye, here was hell last night to play,
  The scream of children, murder cries;
When I came forth at early day,
  I saw old Age with blackened eyes.

Why do I stare at people so,
  Nor watch the little children more,
If one such brutal passions show,
  And joy is all the other's store?

O for the shot in some fierce land,
  A sword or dagger firmly held:
No brutal kick, no mauling hand,
  No horrors of the partly killed.

There is the man with brutal brow,
  The child with hunger's face of care:
The woman – it is something now
  If she lose pride to dress her hair.

I will give children my best hours,
  And of their simple ways will sing:
Just as a bird heeds less old flowers
  And sings his best to buds in spring.

The Old Oak Tree

I sit beneath your leaves, old oak,
   You mighty one of all the trees;
Within whose hollow trunk a man
   Could stable his big horse with ease.

I see your knuckles hard and strong,
   But have no fear they'll come to blows;
Your life is long, and mine is short,
   But which has known the greater woes?

Thou hast not seen starved women here,
   Or man gone mad because ill-fed—
Who stares at stones in city streets,
   Mistaking them for hunks of bread.

Thou hast not felt the shivering backs
   Of homeless children lying down
And sleeping in the cold, night air—
   Like doors and walls, in London town.

Knowing thou hast not known such shame,
   And only storms have come thy way,
Methinks I could in comfort spend
   My summer with thee, day by day.

To lie by day in thy green shade,
   And in thy hollow rest at night;
And through the open doorway see
   The stars turn over leaves of light.

Catharine

We children every morn would wait
For Catharine, at the garden gate;
Behind school-time, her sunny hair
Would melt the master's frown of care,
What time his hand but threatened pain,
Shaking aloft his awful cane;
So here one summer's morn we wait
For Catharine at the garden gate.
To Dave I say – 'There's sure to be
Some coral isle unknown at sea,
And – if I see it first – 'tis mine!
But I'll give it to Catharine.'
'When she grows up,' says Dave to me,
'Some ruler in a far countree,
Where every voice but his is dumb,
Owner of pearls, and gold, and gum,
Will build for her a shining throne,
Higher than his, and near his own;
And he, who would not list before,
Will listen to Catharine, and adore
Her face and form; and,' Dave went on—
When came a man there pale and wan,
Whose face was dark and wet though kind,
He, coming there, seemed like a wind
Whose breath is rain, but will not stop
To give the parched flowers a drop:
'Go, children, to your school,' he said—
'And tell the master Catharine's dead.'

Jenny

Now I grow old, and flowers are weeds,
    I think of days when weeds were flowers;
When Jenny lived across the way,
    And shared with me her childhood hours.

Her little teeth did seem so sharp,
    So bright and bold, when they were shown,
You'd think if passion stirred her she
    Could bite and hurt a man of stone.

Her curls, like golden snakes, would lie
    Upon each shoulder's front, as though
To guard her face on either side—
    They raised themselves when Winds did blow.

How sly they were! I could not see,
    Nor she feel them begin to climb
Across her lips, till there they were,
    To be forced back time after time.

If I could see an Elm in May
    Turn all his dark leaves into pearls,
And shake them in the light of noon—
    That sight had not shamed Jenny's curls.

And, like the hay, I swear her hair
    Was getting golder every day;
Yes, golder when 'twas harvested,
    Under a bonnet stacked away.

Ah, Jenny's gone, I know not where;
    Her face I cannot hope to see;
And every time I think of her
    The world seems one big grave to me.

The Inquest

I took my oath I would inquire,
  Without affection, hate, or wrath,
Into the death of Ada Wright—
  So help me God! I took that oath.

When I went out to see the corpse,
  The four months' babe that died so young,
I judged it was seven pounds in weight,
  And little more than one foot long.

One eye, that had a yellow lid,
  Was shut – so was the mouth, that smiled;
The left eye open, shining bright—
  It seemed a knowing little child.

For as I looked at that one eye,
  It seemed to laugh, and say with glee:
'What caused my death you'll never know—
  Perhaps my mother murdered me.'

When I went into court again,
  To hear the mother's evidence—
It was a love-child, she explained.
  And smiled, for our intelligence.

'Now, Gentlemen of the Jury,' said
  The coroner – 'this woman's child
By misadventure met its death.'
  'Aye, aye,' said we. The mother smiled.

And I could see that child's one eye
  Which seemed to laugh, and say with glee:
'What caused my death you'll never know—
  Perhaps my mother murdered me.'

Mad Poll

There goes mad Poll, dressed in wild flowers,
    Poor, crazy Poll, now old and wan;
Her hair all down, like any child:
    She swings her two arms like a man.

Poor, crazy Poll is never sad,
    She never misses one that dies;
When neighbours show their new-born babes,
    They seem familiar to her eyes.

Her bonnet's always in her hand,
    Or on the ground, and lying near;
She thinks it is a thing for play,
    Or pretty show, and not to wear.

She gives the sick no sympathy,
    She never soothes a child that cries;
She never whimpers, night or day,
    She makes no moans, she makes no sighs.

She talks about some battle old,
    Fought many a day from yesterday;
And when that war is done, her love—
    'Ha, ha!' Poll laughs, and skips away.

Nell Barnes

They lived apart for three long years,
   Bill Barnes and Nell, his wife;
He took his joy from other girls,
   She led a wicked life.

Yet ofttimes she would pass his shop,
   With some strange man awhile;
And, looking, meet her husband's frown
   With her malicious smile.

Until one day, when passing there,
   She saw her man had gone;
And when she saw the empty shop,
   She fell down with a moan.

And when she heard that he had gone
   Five thousand miles away,
And that she'd see his face no more,
   She sickened from that day.

To see his face was health and life,
   And when it was denied,
She could not eat, and broke her heart—
   It was for love she died.

The Bird of Paradise

Here comes Kate Summers who, for gold,
    Takes any man to bed:
'You knew my friend, Nell Barnes,' said she;
    'You knew Nell Barnes – she's dead.

'Nell Barnes was bad on all you men,
    Unclean, a thief as well;
Yet all my life I have not found
    A better friend than Nell.

'So I sat at her side at last,
    For hours, till she was dead;
And yet she had no sense at all
    Of any word I said.

'For all her cry but came to this—
    "Not for the world! Take care:
Don't touch that bird of paradise,
    Perched on the bedpost there!"

'I asked her would she like some grapes,
    Some damsons ripe and sweet;
A custard made with new-laid eggs,
    Or tender fowl to eat.

'I promised I would follow her,
    To see her in her grave;
And buy a wreath with borrowed pence,
    If nothing I could save.

'Yet still her cry but came to this—
    "Not for the world! Take care:
Don't touch that bird of paradise,
    Perched on the bedpost there!"'

The Temper of a Maid

The Swallow dives in yonder air,
The Robin sings with sweetest ease,
The Apple shines among the leaves,
The Leaf is dancing in the breeze;
The Butterfly's on a warm stone,
The Bee is suckled by a flower;
The Wasp's inside a ripe red plum,
The Ant has found his load this hour;
The Squirrel counts and hides his nuts,
The Stoat is on a scent that burns;
The Mouse is nibbling a young shoot,
The Rabbit sits beside his ferns;
The Snake has found a sunny spot,
The Frog and Snail a slimy shade;
But I can find no joy on earth,
All through the temper of a maid.

The Girl is Mad

She changes oft – she laughs and weeps,
    She smiles, and she can frown;
Should tears of sorrow fill her eyes,
    Then laughter shakes them down:
The girl is mad – and yet I love her.

She smiles, and swears her jealousy
    Would tear out my two eyes,
And make me swallow them by force:
    These words are no strong lies,
For she is mad – and yet I love her.

'Ha, ha!' says she; 'I've killed two men,
    And you're the third I'll kill!'
If I keep time with her fierce love,
    'Tis certain that she will:
The girl is mad – and yet I love her.

Raptures

Sing for the sun your lyric, lark,
    Of twice ten thousand notes;
Sing for the moon, you nightingales,
    Whose light shall kiss your throats;
Sing, sparrows, for the soft, warm rain,
    To wet your feathers through;
And, when a rainbow's in the sky,
    Sing you, cuckoo – 'Cuckoo!'

Sing for your five blue eggs, fond thrush,
    By many a leaf concealed;
You starlings, wrens, and blackbirds sing
    In every wood and field;
While I, who fail to give my love
    Long raptures twice as fine,
Will for her beauty breathe this one
    A sigh, that's more divine.

Passion's Greed

His constant wonder keeps him back
    From flying either far or straight;
Confined by thy great beauty here,
    My life is like that butterfly's,
With every source of wonder near.

Let me go burning to my death:
    Nothing can come between our minds
To ease me of this passion's greed:
    We'll bite each other's necks like dogs,
And ask our fingers if we bleed.

A Dream

I met her in the leafy woods,
    Early a summer's night;
I saw her white teeth in the dark,
    There was no better light.

Had she not come up close and made
    Those lilies their light spread,
I had not proved her mouth a rose,
    So round, so fresh, so red.

Her voice was gentle, soft and sweet,
    In words she was not strong;
Yet her low twitter had more charm
    Than any full-mouthed song.

We walked in silence to her cave,
    With but few words to say;
But ever and anon she stopped
    For kisses on the way.

And after every burning kiss
    She laughed and danced around;
Back-bending, with her breasts straight up,
    Her hair it touched the ground.

When we lay down, she held me fast,
    She held me like a leech;
Ho, ho! I know what her red tongue
    Is made for, if not speech.

And what is this, how strange, how sweet!
    Her teeth are made to bite
The man she gives her passion to,
    And not to boast their white.

O night of joy! O morning's grief!
    For when, with passion done,
Rocked on her breast I fell asleep,
    I woke, and lay alone.

The Two Flocks

Where are you going to now, white sheep,
    Walking the green hill-side;
To join that whiter flock on top,
    And share their pride?

Stay where you are, you silly sheep:
    When you arrive up there,
You'll find that whiter flock on top
    Clouds in the air!

Sheep

When I was once in Baltimore,
    A man came up to me and cried,
'Come, I have eighteen hundred sheep,
    And we will sail on Tuesday's tide.

'If you will sail with me, young man,
    I'll pay you fifty shillings down;
These eighteen hundred sheep I take
    From Baltimore to Glasgow town.'

He paid me fifty shillings down,
    I sailed with eighteen hundred sheep;
We soon had cleared the harbour's mouth,
    We soon were in the salt sea deep.

The first night we were out at sea
    Those sheep were quiet in their mind;
The second night they cried with fear—
    They smelt no pastures in the wind.

They sniffed, poor things, for their green fields,
    They cried so loud I could not sleep:
For fifty thousand shillings down
    I would not sail again with sheep.

The Child and the Mariner

A dear old couple my grandparents were,
And kind to all dumb things; they saw in Heaven
The lamb that Jesus petted when a child:
Their faith was never draped by Doubt: to them
Death was a rainbow in Eternity,
That promised everlasting brightness soon.
An old seafaring man was he; a rough
Old man, but kind; and hairy, like the nut
Full of sweet milk. All day on shore he watched
The winds for sailors' wives, and told what ships
Enjoyed fair weather, and what ships had storms;
He watched the sky, and he could tell for sure
What afternoons would follow stormy morns,
If quiet nights would end wild afternoons.
He leapt away from scandal with a roar,
And if a whisper still possessed his mind,
He walked about and cursed it for a plague.
He took offence at Heaven when beggars passed,
And sternly called them back to give them help.

In this old captain's house I lived, and things
That house contained were in ships' cabins once:
Sea-shells and charts and pebbles, model ships;
Green weeds, dried fishes stuffed, and coral stalks;
Old wooden trunks with handles of spliced rope,
With copper saucers full of monies strange,
That seemed the savings of dead men, not touched
To keep them warm since their real owners died;
Strings of red beads, methought were dipped in blood,
And swinging lamps, as though the house might move;
An ivory lighthouse built on ivory rocks,
The bones of fishes and three bottled ships.

And many a thing was there which sailors make
In idle hours, when on long voyages,
Of marvellous patience, to no lovely end.
And on those charts I saw the small black dots
That were called islands, and I knew they had
Turtles and palms, and pirates' buried gold.

There came a stranger to my grandad's house,
The old man's nephew, a seafarer too;
A big, strong able man who could have walked
Twm Barlum's hill all clad in iron mail;
So strong he could have made one man his club
To knock down others – Henry was his name,
No other name was uttered by his kin.
And here he was, in sooth ill-clad, but oh,
Thought I, what secrets of the sea are his!
This man knows coral islands in the sea,
And dusky girls heart-broken for white men;
This sailor knows of wondrous lands afar,
More rich than Spain, when the Phoenicians shipped
Silver for common ballast, and they saw
Horses at silver mangers eating grain;
This man has seen the wind blow up a mermaid's hair
Which, like a golden serpent, reared and stretched
To feel the air away beyond her head.
He begged my pennies, which I gave with joy—
He will most certainly return some time
A self-made king of some new land, and rich.
Alas that he, the hero of my dreams,
Should be his people's scorn; for they had rose
To proud command of ships, whilst he had toiled
Before the mast for years, and well content;
Him they despised, and only Death could bring
A likeness in his face to show like them.
For he drank all his pay, nor went to sea
As long as ale was easy got on shore.

Now, in his last long voyage he had sailed
From Plymouth Sound to where sweet odours fan
The Cingalese at work, and then back home—
But came not near my kin till pay was spent.
He was not old, yet seemed so; for his face
Looked like the drowned man's in the morgue, when it
Has struck the wooden wharves and keels of ships.
And all his flesh was pricked with Indian ink,
His body marked as rare and delicate
As dead men struck by lightning under trees,
And pictured with fine twigs and curled ferns;
Chains on his neck and anchors on his arms;
Rings on his fingers, bracelets on his wrist;
And on his breast the *Jane* of Appledore
Was schooner rigged, and in full sail at sea.
He could not whisper with his strong hoarse voice,
No more than could a horse creep quietly;
He laughed to scorn the men that muffled close
For fear of wind, till all their neck was hid,
Like Indian corn wrapped up in long green leaves;
He knew no flowers but seaweeds brown and green,
He knew no birds but those that followed ships.
Full well he knew the water-world; he heard
A grander music there than we on land,
When organ shakes a church; swore he would make
The sea his home, though it was always roused
By such wild storms as never leave Cape Horn;
Happy to hear the tempest grunt and squeal
Like pigs heard dying in a slaughterhouse.
A true-born mariner, and this his hope—
His coffin would be what his cradle was,
A boat to drown in and be sunk at sea;
To drown at sea and lie a dainty corpse
Salted and iced in Neptune's larder deep.
This man despised small coasters, fishing-smacks;

He scorned those sailors who at night and morn
Can see the coast, when in their little boats
They go a six days' voyage and are back
Home with their wives for every Sabbath day.
Much did he talk of tankards of old beer,
And bottled stuff he drank in other lands,
Which was a liquid fire like Hell to gulp,
But Paradise to sip.

              And so he talked;
Nor did those people listen with more awe
To Lazarus – whom they had seen stone dead—
Than did we urchins to that seaman's voice.
He many a tale of wonder told: of where,
At Argostoli, Cephalonia's sea
Ran over the earth's lip in heavy floods;
And then again of how the strange Chinese
Conversed much as our homely Blackbirds sing.
He told us how he sailed in one old ship
Near that volcano Martinique, whose power
Shook like dry leaves the whole Caribbean seas;
And made the sun set in a sea of fire
Which only half was his; and dust was thick
On deck, and stones were pelted at the mast.
So, as we walked along, that seaman dropped
Into my greedy ears such words that sleep
Stood at my pillow half the night perplexed.
He told how isles sprang up and sank again,
Between short voyages, to his amaze;
How they did come and go, and cheated charts;
Told how a crew was cursed when one man killed
A bird that perched upon a moving barque;
And how the sea's sharp needles, firm and strong,
Ripped open the bellies of big, iron ships;
Of mighty icebergs in the Northern seas,

That haunt the far horizon like white ghosts.
He told of waves that lift a ship so high
That birds could pass from starboard unto port
Under her dripping keel.

                              Oh, it was sweet
To hear that seaman tell such wondrous tales:
How deep the sea in parts, that drowned men
Must go a long way to their graves and sink
Day after day, and wander with the tides.
He spake of his own deeds; of how he sailed
One summer's night along the Bosphorus,
And he – who knew no music like the wash
Of waves against a ship, or wind in shrouds—
Heard then the music on that woody shore
Of nightingales, and feared to leave the deck,
He thought 'twas sailing into Paradise.

To hear these stories all we urchins placed
Our pennies in that seaman's ready hand;
Until one morn he signed for a long cruise,
And sailed away – we never saw him more.
Could such a man sink in the sea unknown?
Nay, he had found a land with something rich,
That kept his eyes turned inland for his life.
'A damn bad sailor and a landshark too,
No good in port or out' – my grandad said.

The Poet

When I went down past Charing Cross,
　A plain and simple man was I;
I might have been no more than air,
　Unseen by any mortal eye.

But, Lord in Heaven, had I the power
　To show my inward spirit there,
Then what a pack of human hounds
　Had hunted me, to strip me bare.

A human pack, ten thousand strong,
　All in full cry to bring me down;
All greedy for my magic robe,
　All crazy for my burning crown.

Thunderstorms

My mind has thunderstorms,
   That brood for heavy hours:
Until they rain me words,
   My thoughts are drooping flowers
And sulking, silent birds.

Yet come, dark thunderstorms,
   And brood your heavy hours;
For when you rain me words,
   My thoughts are dancing flowers
And joyful singing birds.

Killed in Action
(Edward Thomas)

Happy the man whose home is still
   In Nature's green and peaceful ways;
To wake and hear the birds so loud,
   That scream for joy to see the sun
Is shouldering past a sullen cloud.

And we have known those days, when we
   Would wait to hear the cuckoo first;
When you and I, with thoughtful mind,
   Would help a bird to hide her nest,
For fear of other hands less kind.

But thou, my friend, art lying dead:
   War, with its hell-born childishness,
Has claimed thy life, with many more:
   The man that loved this England well,
And never left it once before.

Francis Thompson

Thou hadst no home, and thou couldst see
   In every street the windows' light:
   Dragging thy limbs about all night,
No window kept a light for thee.

However much thou wert distressed,
   Or tired of moving, and felt sick,
   Thy life was on the open deck—
Thou hadst no cabin for thy rest.

Thy barque was helpless 'neath the sky,
   No pilot thought thee worth his pains
   To guide for love or money gains—
Like phantom ships the rich sailed by.

Thy shadow mocked thee night and day,
   Thy life's companion, it alone;
   It did not sigh, it did not moan,
But mocked thy moves in every way.

In spite of all, the mind had force,
   And, like a stream whose surface flows
   The wrong way when a strong wind blows,
It underneath maintained its course.

Oft didst thou think thy mind would flower
   Too late for good, as some bruised tree
   That blooms in Autumn, and we see
Fruit not worth picking, hard and sour.

Some poets *feign* their wounds and scars:
  If they had known real suffering hours,
  They'd show, in place of Fancy's flowers,
More of Imagination's stars.

So, if thy fruits of Poesy
  Are rich, it is at this dear cost—
  That they were nipt by Sorrow's frost,
In nights of homeless misery.

Ale

Now do I hear thee weep and groan,
  Who hast a comrade sunk at sea?
Then quaff thee of my good old ale,
  And it will raise him up for thee;
Thou'lt think as little of him then
As when he moved with living men.

If thou hast hopes to move the world,
  And every effort it doth fail,
Then to thy side call Jack and Jim,
  And bid them drink with thee good ale;
So may the world, that would not hear,
Perish in hell with all your care.

One quart of good old ale, and I
  Feel then what life immortal is:
The brain is empty of all thought,
  The heart is brimming o'er with bliss;
Time's first child, Life, doth live; but Death,
The second, hath not yet his breath.

Give me a quart of good old ale,
  Am I a homeless man on earth?
Nay, I want not your roof and quilt,
  I'll lie warm at the moon's cold hearth,
No grumbling ghost to grudge my bed,
His grave, ha! ha! holds up my head.

Come, Honest Boys

Ye who have nothing to conceal,
    Come, honest boys, and drink with me;
Come, drink with me the sparkling ale,
    And we'll not whisper calumny,
But laugh with all the power we can;
    But all pale schemers who incline
To rise above your fellow man,
    Touch not the sparkling ale or wine.

Give me strong ale to fire my blood,
    Content me with a lot that's bad;
That is to me both drink and food,
    And warms me though I am ill-clad;
A pot of ale, man owns the world:
    The poet hears his songs all sung,
Inventor sees his patents sold,
    The painter sees his pictures hung.

The creeds remind us oft of Death;
    But man's best creed is to forget
Death all the hours that he takes breath,
    And quaff the sparkling ale, and let
Creeds shout until they burst their lungs;
    For what is better than to be
A-drinking ale and singing songs,
    In summer, under some green tree?

They're Taxing Ale Again

Ale's no false liar; though his mind
    Has thoughts that are not clear,
His honest heart speaks boldly out,
    Without reserve or fear.
Though shaky as that bird the bat,
    In its first flight at night,
Yet still old Ale will stand his ground
    For either wrong or right.

Though Ale is poor, he's no man's slave,
    He'll neither fawn nor lick;
He'd clap proud monarchs on the back,
    And call them Ned or Dick.
They're taxing Ale again, I hear,
    A penny more the can:
They're taxing poor old Ale again,
    The only honest man.

The Soul's Destroyer

London! What utterance the mind finds here!
In its academy of art, more rich
Than that proud temple which made Ophir poor,
And the resources famed of Sheba's Queen.
And its museums, hoarding up the past,
With their rare bones of animals extinct;
And woven stuffs embroidered by the East
Ere other hemispheres could know that Peace
Had trophies pleasanter to win than War;
The great man, wrought to very life in stone—
Of genius, that raises spirits that
It cannot lay until their will is wrought—
Till in their eyes we seek to wander awed,
Lost in the mind's immensity, to find
The passage barred, the spirit gone away.
And not without sweet sounds to hear: as I
Have heard the music, like a hiding child,
Low chuckling its delight behind a wall,
Which, with a sudden burst and joyous cry,
Out leapt and on my heart threw its sweet weight—
When strolling in the palace-bounded parks
Of our great city on a summer's morn.
Now, one who lives for long in London town
Doth feel his love divided 'tween the two—
A city's noise and Nature's quiet call:
His heart is as a mother's, that can hear
Voices of absent children o'er the sea
Calling to her, and children's words at home.
E'en when old Thames rolls in his fog, and men
Are lost, and only blind men know their way;
When Morning borrows of the Evening's lamps,
Or when bewildered millions battle home

With stifled throats, and eyes that burn with pain—
Still are there lovers faithful to such moods.
But in thy slums, where I have seen men gaunt,
In their vile prisons where they wander starved
Without a jailer for their common needs—
Heard children whimper to their mother's moan;
Where rich ones, had they love, with willing hands,
Have privilege to win their godhead soon
By charity that's needless in new realms—
Oh, who can love thy slums with starving ones!
Where children live, like flowers in Ocean's dells,
Unvisited by light or balmy wind:
As daffodils, that plead with their sweet smiles
Our charity for their rude father March.
Thy place is in the slums, O Charity,
These are thy churches for thy visitings;
The charity that seeks is nobler far
Than charity that must at home be sought.
This London served my life for full five years.

In sheer disgust to know intemperance
And poverty, and leaning to the sot
Who lays this precious intellect to sleep,
As though no beauty was in all the world,
With heaven and earth scarce worthy of a thought,
And helpless grown of every future joy—
Methought return to Nature might restore
Youth's early peace and faith's simplicity.
Though Hope be an illusion, yet our life
Were never so bewildered as without it;
An April day of sunny promises
When we are suffering actual cold and want,
And child of Discontent – without such hints
Of coming joy Life's name were Vanity.
Hopeless had I become, a wreck of men;

A derelict that neither sinks nor floats,
Is drifting out of sight of heaven and earth,
Not of the ways of men, but *in* their ways.
And there lived one, now to another wed,
Whom I had secret wish to look upon,
With sweet remembrance of our earlier years.
Her presence then a pool of deep repose
To break Life's dual run from Innocence
To Manhood, and from Manhood unto Age,
And a sweet pause for all my murmuring;
Until a way, for which is no account,
Set me to run again, and she received
Into her favour one who was my friend.
Oft had I mourned those days for ever gone
We went together side by side to school,
Together had our holidays in fields
Made golden by June's buttercups; in woods,
Where under ferns fresh pulled I buried her,
And called her forth like Lazarus from the grave;
She'd laughing come, to shake her curls until
Methought to hear full half a hundred bells.
A grown-up world took playful notice soon,
Made me feel shame that grew a greater love;
She was more chary of her laughter then,
And more subdued her voice, as soft and sweet
As Autumn's, blowing through his golden reeds.
In her sweet sympathies she was a woman
When scarcely she was more than child in years;
And yet one angry moment parted us,
And days of longing never joined us more.

One morning I awoke with lips gone dry,
The tongue an obstacle to choke the throat,
And aching body weighted with more heads
Than Pluto's dog; the features hard and set,

As though encased in a plaster cast;
With limbs all sore through falling here and there
To drink the various ales the Borough kept
From London Bridge to Newington, and streets
Adjoining, alleys, lanes obscure from them,
Then thought of home and of the purer life,
Of Nature's air, and having room to breathe,
A sunny sky, green field, and water's sound;
Of peaceful rivers not yet fretful grown
As when their mouths have tasted Ocean's salt;
And where the rabbits sit amid their ferns,
Or leap, to flash the white of their brown tails.
Less time a grey crow picks the partridge clean,
I was apparelled, and, with impulse that
Was wonderful in one of many sprees,
Went onward rapidly from street to street.
I still had vision clear of Nature's face,
Though muddled in my senses to the ways
And doings of the days and nights before.
I heard the city roaring like a beast
That's wronged by one that feared an open strife
And triumphed by his cunning as I walked.
It followed on for hours with rushing sound,
As some great cataract had burst all bounds
And was oncoming with its mingled pines—
The fallen sentinels – to choke the sea.
Once in awhile the sound, though not less near,
Seemed distant, barred by dwellings closely joined,
But at a corner's turn heard full again;
Yet lessened soon and sure to softer ways
Of a low murmuring – as though it found
Anger was vain, and coaxed for my return.
All day walked I, and that same night, I scorned
The shelter of a house, lay peaceful down
Beneath the glorious stars; beneath that nest

Of singing stars men call the Milky Way;
Thought it, maybe, the way that spirits take,
And heavenly choir to sing triumphal march
For dead men for the New Jerusalem.
I was alone: had left the Borough in
Safe care of my old cronies, who would keep
Its reputation from becoming changed
Into a quiet neighbourhood.

As with a shipwrecked seaman cast ashore,
And carried to a land's interior
By the rude natives, there to work and slave
Quarries and mines of their barbaric king;
Who after years escapes his servitude
To wander lost, at last to see before
Him mountains which he climbs to see beyond,
When on their top he stands beholds the sea!
And, wonders more, a fleet of friendly flags
Lying at anchor for his signalling—
Such joy a hundred times a day was mine
To see at every bend of the road the face
Of Nature different. And oft I sat
To hear the lark from his first twitter pass
To greater things as he soared nearer heaven;
Or to the throstle, singing nearer home,
With less of that abandon and wild fire,
But steady, like a sheltered light from wind.
What joy was mine, sweet Nature, to return!
The flower so wild, reared on thine own pure milk
Of dew and rain, and by thy sunbeams warmed,
Speckled the green with light of various hues;
The hawthorn it caught slippery Mercury,
And smothered him to smell of where he'd been;
And everything that had a voice made sound,
The speechless things were gladsome in dumb smiles.

It was a day of rest in heaven, which seemed
A blue grass field thick dotted with white tents
Which Life slept late in, as 'twere holiday.
Yon lord or squire in his great house,
Who himself busies guessing all his days
The age of horses and the weight of hogs,
The breed of hounds – not such as he has held
The ear to Nature's quiet heart-beat. No;
He overlooks the flower to spy the fox,
Ignores the lark's song for the halloing horn,
Nor hears the echo of that horn he loves—
Not such as he is rich in Nature's stores.
I've seen proud Autumn in more gold arrayed,
Ere cold October strips and blows him bare,
Than ever delved from earth or ta'en from water's wash;
More pearls seen scattered to a summer's morn
Than Ocean e'er possessed in depths or out,
Though in his water's workshop – like a slave.
Who sees a cobweb strung with dew pearls, sees
A finer work than jewelled crowns of gold.
Few are thy friends, sweet Nature, in these days,
But thou art still the Solitary's love.
The glory of the river's long since gone,
The land is sped and beauty unrevealed.
The motor-car goes humming down the road,
Like some huge bee that warns us from its way.
On, on, we speed by fire on slippery rails,
And earth goes spinning back from whence we came,
And through the trees, or on the hills' smooth tops
That cut the heaven clean the day's one orb
Goes with us till he sinks before the dark,
Clouds towering with him, to his back and front;
We speed our way through tunnels under ground,
Where one sees naught but faces of his kind.
Let others praise thy parts, sweet Nature; I

Who cannot know the barley from the oats,
Nor call the bird by note, nor name a star,
Claim thy heart's fullness through the face of things.
The lonely shepherd in his hut at night
Will dream of Beauty in the feverous towns,
Of Love and Gaiety, of Song and Dance;
With fore-paws on his master's crook, the dog
Sleeps dreaming his life's duty though his flocks
Are countless, and the hills on which they roam:
So faithful I to thee, like shepherd's dog,
To follow thee with joy in all thy moods,
As docile as the lamb that Una led.
When man shall stand apart from this dear world,
And have his vision's manifold increase,
To see it rolled at morning when the sun
Makes lamps of domes and lighthouses of fanes,
With its green fields, blue waters, and its hills,
And smiling valleys filled with brooks and flowers;
To hear the music of the world once his,
Singing in unison with other spheres—
He shall exclaim, 'I have God's second heaven
Ere I have known the wonder of His first.'

Six days had gone, and I at length near home,
Where toil the Cymry deep in sunless pits,
And emptying all their hills to warm the world,
Soon saw familiar scenes, and saw no change:
The rookery, where never silence seemed—
For every hour seemed it to be disturbed
By strange new-comers, aliens to invade;
Or, maybe, known ones bringing envied stores
Which stay-at-homes would clamour to divide.
And near that rookery a river ran,
And over it a bridge too small for piers;
Another crossing, of irregular stones,

Was seen, which in the springtime flooded o'er;
And I had heard the river tell their number,
And spell like letters of an alphabet,
That it would never tire repeating day
And night. When young I oft had bared my feet
To go from bank to bank, leapt stone to stone,
My ankles wetted on a sunken one.
Beyond the bridge was seen the village spire—
My courage failed. I feared to see in life
Her who was now the heroine of dreams,
And sweet familiar of my solitude
And silence, and whose shadowy hand kept full
The cup of memory; and in such mood
Entered an inn, to seek that courage which
Makes man abuse his friends, and wish them foes;
Or puts unnatural pity in his mind
To help strange ones, forgetful of his own.
Not one known face had met my own, or voice
To recognise, until that moment came;
And then such sight to see that had the man
Been other than he was had not surprised:
He who had wed my love stood shaking there
While to his lips another held the glass
Which his own hand lacked power to raise unspilled;
And there stood he, in manner of a beast
That's drinking from a trough, but more the greed.
We greeted as old friends; few moments passed
When I inquired of her, in casual way,
On which a fearful change came over him:
'Why, she hath filled the house with merry men
To mock her husband,' he replied, and turned
His head in fear. And well I knew his thoughts,
And of such demons in a drunkard's dream,
The sleepless dream that wearies flesh and brain.
This curse of drink, in village and in town,

70

The curse of nations, their decline and fall,
Ere they can question purpose of this life;
And so 'twill be until the mind is reared
To see the beauty that is in the world,
Of science, art, and Nature at all times;
To know that temperance and sobriety
Is truer joy – e'en though the grave ends all—
Than an unnatural merriment that brings
A thousand tortures for its hundred joys.
He now seemed worse and moved about the room,
And many a sound of triumph, anguish made,
Though from his unseen foes receiving knocks
And giving in return. We stood in awe!
One looked at me and said: 'He should be home,
And we are much to blame for him; wouldst thou
See him safe there? for none can censure thee.'
'Nay, I would rather tread his threshold floor,
And dare all devils of his fancy there,
Than front his wife and children innocent.'
As some lone hunter might at sunrise see,
Upon the margent of a woodland pool,
Huge prints of something alien to his lore,
And know not if 'twere fowl or beast, or freak
Of man – so awed, amazed I stood; until
He grew more calm, and then we coaxed him home.

We reached his home, a cottage lone and small
And such a place was my ideal to live,
Where I might walk it round, touch its four sides,
Free to the sun in every latitude,
Unto the first and final look on Earth.
And at its door three little Aprils played,
Three little children, little Aprils all,
So full were they of April's strife and love;
Who, when they saw us coming, ran to meet us,

71

To make a bridal entry with their laughter;
But saw a stranger, and their father cold,
Fell back, and followed hushed, a funeral train.
Sure, thought I, our whole duty is to leave
Our children's state exalted 'bove our own:
Equipping them with kinder thoughts than ours,
And they do likewise in their day; so through
The generations to at last attain
The climax of our mortal purity.
Had I so failed to these poor little ones
If she and I were sharing of their lives?
We entered, and we stood before her face,
And it was stern, as woe affects the man,
Not that sweet resignation of her sex.
She looked on me as one unjustly served,
A look regretful, part resigned, as if
Some retribution was my right to claim.
Her once blue sapphire eyes had not a gleam,
As they would never smile or weep again,
And had no light to draw the waters up
Which staled upon her heart. To me all seemed
So plain: that she had loved without avail,
And reasoned, then had widowed her own self,
A widowhood in which Death claimed no part.
All night he raved, and in his madness died.
And I have seen his death-look on a beast
Baring the teeth 'twas powerless to use
Against a foe of greater strength, and there
Lay dead, intentions hatefully revealed.
Such his dread look: the vicious show of teeth
Made bare in hatred to his unseen foes.
Such is this drink that fathers half our sins;
It makes a simple one responsible
For deeds which memory makes no count to save,
And proves man guilty in his innocence.

When he shall stand before his judging God
He needs must answer charges strange to him
And his own mind to One who sees all things;
And what He sees, He never can forget.
May God have mercy on our frailties!
Sure we, though set a thousand years of pain,
Nor once should murmur at vicissitude,
Yet ill deserve those promises fulfilled
Of an eternity of bliss with Him;
And who can know the thoughts of him in hell,
Who sacrificed eternity of joy
To gratify this little life on earth!
Were't not for God Almighty's mercy, trees
Would 'scape the thunderbolt, th' unfeeling rocks
The lightning's blast; all ills would fall on man,
Who hides his conscience in a covered cage,
As dumb and silent as a moulting bird.

A Poet's Epitaph

Here lie the bones of Davies – William,
   Who always called the moon Phoebe,
And Phoebus always called the sun,
   And must, therefore, a poet be.

'Twas one to him to sing in heaven,
   Or howl with demons in hell's pits,
To make himself at home, for he
   Was homeless here by starts and fits.

The world cursed him, and he cursed it,
   Till Death with dirt his throat did fill;
If e'er he wakes, he'll curse again,
   And worse – this Davies, William – will.

His granny oft foretold his fate,
   How he a ne'er-do-well would be;
'Twas well, maybe, she never heard
   The rascal call the moon Phoebe.

His grandad said – 'He is a rogue.'
   'Not me, grandad,' said William's brother.
'Why, thou art fool!' their grandad roared.
   'Nay, young and simple both,' said mother.

The Autobiography of a Super-tramp

W.H. Davies

ISBN 978-1-908946-07-2
£8.99 • Paperback

'I have read it through from beginning to end and would have read more had there been any more to read.'
– George Bernard Shaw

The Autobiography of a Super-tramp
W.H. DAVIES

Young Emma

W.H. Davies

ISBN 978-1-910409-45-9
£8.99 • Paperback

'An extraordinary memoir destined to become a classic'
– Publishers Weekly

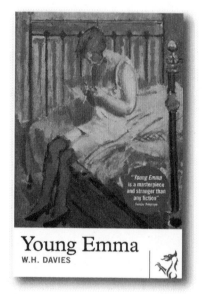

"Young Emma is a masterpiece and stranger than any fiction"
Sunday Telegraph

Young Emma
W.H. DAVIES

PARTHIAN

Related titles

Poetry 1900–2000
One hundred poets from Wales
EDITED BY MEIC STEPHENS

Poetry 1900-2000

Edited by Meic Stephens

ISBN 978-1-902638-88-1
£15.99 • Paperback

'This anthology is a wonderful compendium
of good poems and poets worth meeting,
many worth returning to again and again.'
– *New Welsh Review*

Edward Thomas & Wales

Edited by Jeff Towns

ISBN 978-1-91-268112-9
£8.99 • Paperback

'A judicious and telling anthology of the
writings of the writings of one of the three
great poetic Thomases of Wales.'
– Jon Gower

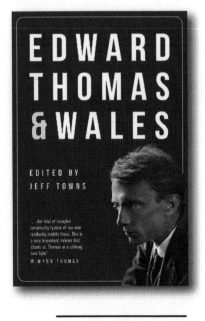

EDWARD THOMAS & WALES

EDITED BY
JEFF TOWNS

...the kind of complex
personality typical of our own
restlessly mobile times. This is
a very important release that
shows us Thomas in a striking
new light'
M. WYNN THOMAS

 PARTHIAN

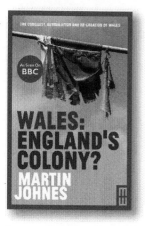

WALES: ENGLAND'S COLONY?

Martin Johnes

From the very beginnings of Wales, its people have defined themselves against their large neighbour. This book tells the fascinating story of an uneasy and unequal relationship between two nations living side-by-side.

PB / £8.99
978-1-912681-41-9

RHYS DAVIES: A WRITER'S LIFE

Meic Stephens

Rhys Davies (1901-78) was among the most dedicated, prolific and accomplished of Welsh prose writers. This is his first full biography.

'This is a delightful book, which is itself a social history in its own right, and funny.'
– The Spectator

PB / £11.99
978-1-912109-96-8

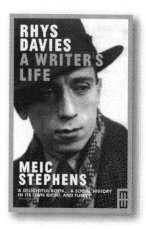

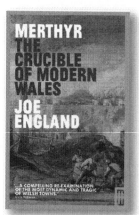

MERTHYR, THE CRUCIBLE OF MODERN WALES

Joe England

Merthyr Tydfil was the town where the future of a country was forged: a thriving, struggling surge of people, industry, democracy and ideas. This book assesses an epic history of Merthyr from 1760 to 1912 through the focus of a fresh and thoroughly convincing perspective.

PB / £18.99
978-1-913640-05-7

TO HEAR THE SKYLARK'S SONG

Huw Lewis

To Hear the Skylark's Song is a memoir about how Aberfan survived and eventually thrived after the terrible disaster of the 21st of October 1966.

'A thoughtful and passionate memoir, moving and respectful.'
– Tessa Hadley

PB / £8.99
978-1-912109-72-2

ROCKING THE BOAT

Angela V. John

This insightful and revealing collection of essays focuses on seven Welsh women who, in a range of imaginative ways, resisted the status quo in Wales, England and beyond during the nineteenth and twentieth centuries.

PB / £11.99
978-1-912681-44-0

TURNING THE TIDE

Angela V. John

This rich biography tells the remarkable tale of Margaret Haig Thomas (1883-1958) who became the second Viscountess Rhondda. She was a Welsh suffragette, held important posts during the First World War and survived the sinking of the *Lusitania*.

PB / £17.99
978-1-909844-72-8

BRENDA CHAMBERLAIN, ARTIST & WRITER

Jill Piercy

The first full-length biography of Brenda Chamberlain chronicles the life of an artist and writer whose work was strongly affected by the places she lived, most famously Bardsey Island and the Greek island of Hydra.

PB / £11.99
978-1-912681-06-8

PARTHIAN Parthian Voices

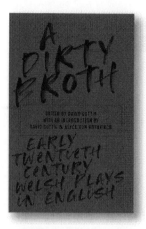

A DIRTY BROTH: EARLY-TWENTIETH CENTURY WELSH PLAYS IN ENGLISH

VOLUME 1 OF TWENTIETH-CENTURY WELSH PLAYS IN ENGLISH

Edited by David Cottis

This anthology, the first in a series of three, brings together three plays from the beginnings of Welsh playwriting in English.

PB /£14.99
978-1-912681-71-6

A LADDER OF WORDS: MID-TWENTIETH CENTURY WELSH PLAYS IN ENGLISH

VOLUME 2 OF TWENTIETH-CENTURY WELSH PLAYS IN ENGLISH

Edited by David Cottis

A Ladder of Words explores the period either side of the Second World War, a time when Welsh playwrights enjoyed unprecedented commercial success.

PB / £14.99
978-1-913640-04-0

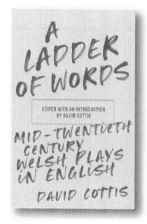

SAINTS AND LODGERS: THE POEMS OF W.H. DAVIES

Selected with an introduction by Jonathan Edwards

William Henry Davies (1871–1940) was a Welsh poet and writer. He was also a traveller and adventurer. In this collection he emerges as a poet of people, who never turns away from the suffering or the beauty of the saints and lodgers among whom he lives.

PB / £9.99
978-1-912681-34-1